L'ATELIER

THE

~ 1(

short stories

ABOUT

THE OLYMPIC GAMES

Who doesn't like stories? Everyone loves stories!

The 100 short stories are designed to help you discover or rediscover
anecdotes, records or unusual and juicy information !

A way to stimulate your curiosity and entertain yourself
Want to improve your general knowledge while having fun ?
You've come to the right place !

Dear readers, have fun !

The modern Olympic Games were re-established in 1896 in Athens, Greece.

However, the original Summer Olympics date back to about 776 BC.

#1

The Olympic fire, which burns throughout the game, is lit atop Mount Olympus in Greece and transported to the host city of the games.

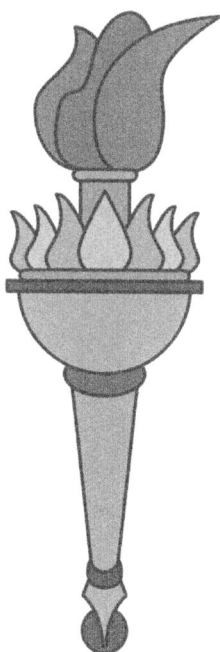

The first modern Olympic Games included only nine sports, while the 2020 Summer Games in Tokyo included 33 different sports.

#3

The women were allowed to participate in the Olympic Games only in 1900 in Paris.

Romanian gymnast Nadia Comăneci was the first athlete to earn a perfect score of 10 in Olympic competition in 1976 in Montreal.

#5

During the 1968 Olympic Games in Mexico City, the American sprinter Tommie Smith and the American long jumper John Carlos raised their black-gloved fists in protest during the medal ceremony to protest against racial injustices in the United States.

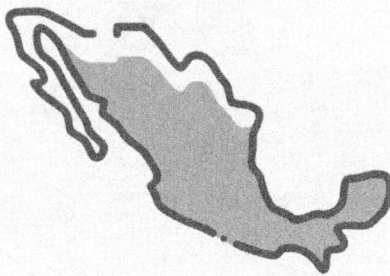

MÉXICO

The most gold medals won by an individual athlete at a single Olympic Games is held by American swimmer Michael Phelps, who won eight gold medals in Beijing in 2008.

#7

The Olympic Games include an official anthem, "Ode to Joy", extracted from the Ninth Symphony by Ludwig van Beethoven.

The Olympic Games were suspended during the first and second world wars.

#9

The 1956 Games in Melbourne were the first to be broadcast on television on a large scale.

The basketball tournament at the Olympic Games has been won by the United States team at every summer games since 1936, except in 1972 in Munich.

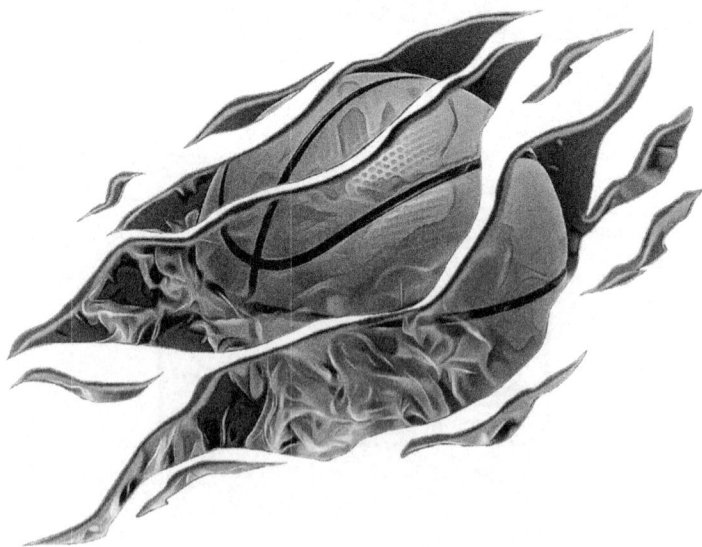

#11

The 2020 Summer Olympics in Tokyo have been rescheduled for 2021 due to the COVID-19 pandemic.

PANDEMIC

#12

The highest number of gold medals won by a nation at a single Olympic Games is held by the United States, which won 46 gold medals in Los Angeles in 1984.

#13

The 2014 Winter Olympics in Sochi cost over $50 billion, making it the most expensive Games in history.

The 2024 Summer Olympics in Paris will be the first to feature a skateboarding event.

#15

The Olympic Games were banned by the Roman power in 393 AD because of their link with the Greek religion.

The Games were restored only in 1896.

Olympic athletes must be at least 16 years old to participate in the Summer Games and at least 15 years old for the Winter Games.

#17

The first Summer Olympic Games hosted by an Asian city took place in 1964 in Tokyo.

#18

German swimmer Paul Biedermann broke the world record in 2009 by wearing a polyurethane swimsuit. This led to a review of the rules regarding the technology used for competition clothing.

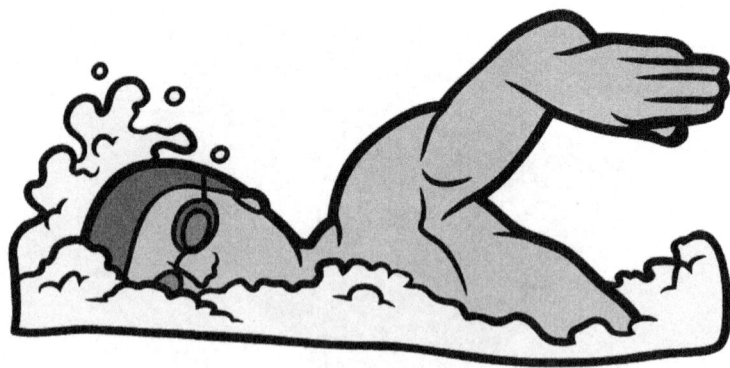

#19

The oldest Olympic athlete in history is Oscar Swahn, who won a silver medal in rifle shooting at the age of 72 at the 1912 Stockholm Olympics.

Gymnast Simone Biles is the first woman to perform a double front somersault with a ½ turn double rotation at the 2016 Rio Olympics.

#21

Sprint runner Usain Bolt is considered one of the fastest sprinters of all time, winning nine Olympic gold medals.

The Olympic Games have been cancelled only 5 times. Once in Berlin because of the First World War (1916). Then on two other occasions, in London and Tokyo, this time during the Second World War (1940 and 1944).

On these last two occasions, both the Summer and Winter Games were cancelled.

#23

For the first time in history, in 2000, North Korea and South Korea parade together at the opening ceremony of the Games, and the athletes of both countries are dressed in the same clothes and stand behind a single flag.

The feat was achieved again in Pyeongchang in South Korea in 2018.

#24

The Olympic Games of Moscow (1980) and Los Angeles (1984) take place in the middle of the Cold War between the USSR and the United States. It all starts with a call for a boycott, from the Americans, in front of the presence of the games on Soviet soil. They do not go to the Soviet Union, under the pretext that they are protesting against the invasion of Afghanistan. 4 years, after having seen almost half of the world refusing to come to Moscow, the Soviet Union does not go to Los Angeles. About fifteen countries from the communist bloc also follow the movement.

#25

The Olympic Games of Moscow are also marked by the victory celebration of the Polish athlete Wladyslaw Kozakiewicz. The spectators of the Lenin stadium, who supported the Soviet Konstantin Volkov, have done everything to disconcert him. They used whistles and shouted insults at him throughout the competition, in order to break his concentration. Once declared the winner, he then addressed the furious audience with a smile, but above all with a memorable arm of honor.

#26

The 1968 Mexico City Games were marked by the American civil rights movement. The Games take place a few months after the assassination of Martin Luther King. The African-American athletes take advantage of the visibility of the games to show their opposition to the racial segregation which rages in the United States. The athletes Tommie Smith and John Carlos go even to use the gloved fist of the Black Panthers to celebrate their victory on the podium, during the raising of the flag of the United States and the American anthem.

#27

Abebe Bikila was unknown before he arrived at the 1960 Rome Games, but he would become a sports legend. Bikila, a soldier in the Ethiopian army, was a last-minute replacement for an injured teammate and had to run the marathon without notice.

But the most memorable part of the story was when Bikila decided to run the 42.195-kilometer course barefoot. The reason? His new shoes gave him blisters.

#28

The 1996 Atlanta Olympics are best remembered for the blood that flowed. Unfortunately, the Olympic village is the scene of a bombing. The explosion makes two dead and more than 100 wounded. Richard Jewel, a security guard, is the first intervening on the scene. He quickly became a national hero.

#29

On September 5, 1972, in response to the violence and treatment of residents on Palestinian territory, the terrorist group "Black September" broke into the Olympic Village, killing two members of the Israeli team and then taking nine hostages. The group demanded the release of 234 Palestinian prisoners, held in Israel. In the ensuing battle for their release, the nine Israeli hostages all lost their lives, as did five of the terrorists and a German policeman.

#30

The Olympic Games of Berlin of 1936 take place in an extremely tense historical context. Germany, under the control of Adolph Hitler and the Nazis since 1933, frightens the whole world. On August 3, 1936, in the titanic "Olympiastadion" of Berlin, more than 100 000 spectators are gathered. During these Games, Owens wins in total 4 events: the 100 m, the 200 m, the relay 4 x 100m and the long jump. Hitler, furious to see a Black triumph, would have refused to shake his hand and would have even left the stadium.

#31

During the 1972 Games, the weightlifter David Rigert is the favorite in his middleweight category. Unfortunately for him, the things do not happen at all as foreseen; he misses completely his tournament and does not leave with any medal. The Soviet will then completely lose his footing, he will hit his head against the walls, pulling out handfuls of hair. To calm him down, it was necessary the intervention of the other competitors before he seriously injured himself. 4 years later, he will become Olympic champion.

Also in 1972, the American Mark Spitz won 7 medals in only 8 days, beating the world record in each event. Journalists asked him what his secret was. The swimmer humorously retorts that it is thanks to his moustache. It prevents water from entering his mouth and therefore saves him time. A joke that his Russian competitors took seriously, who one year later presented themselves in the pools with a moustache!

#33

During the Olympic Games of 1972, in Munich, a huge polemic bursts during the final of basketball between the United States and Russia. At 3s of the end, the Americans take the advantage but the referee whistles 1s before the end of the game because the Russians had asked for a time-out which was forgotten. A new throw-in is then made but the Russians don't score and the Americans are champions. But an official decides, against all odds, to replay these 3 seconds because the clock was wrong!
The Russians finally manage to score!

#34

In 1912, Dick Williams was on board the Titanic. The American survived the disaster and refused to have his legs amputated even though they had been in the icy water for hours. This decision was the right one, because one year later, Williams won his first Davis Cup. He won 6 in total, and one year after this victory, he won the US Open. In 1924, he even became Olympic champion in mixed doubles with Hazel Wightman.

The Olympics are a way to showcase your creativity and culture to the world. The British have brilliantly seized this opportunity in 2012 by integrating, in the opening ceremony of the Games, two world-famous symbols of their country: James Bond and Mr. Bean. Daniel Craig, the emblematic actor of James Bond, appears in parachute above the Olympic stadium, a few seconds after the broadcasting of a clip in which Queen Elizabeth II and the secret agent meet the time of a helicopter flight.

#36

In ancient Greece, athletes did not care about sponsors, protection or fashion.
They competed naked!

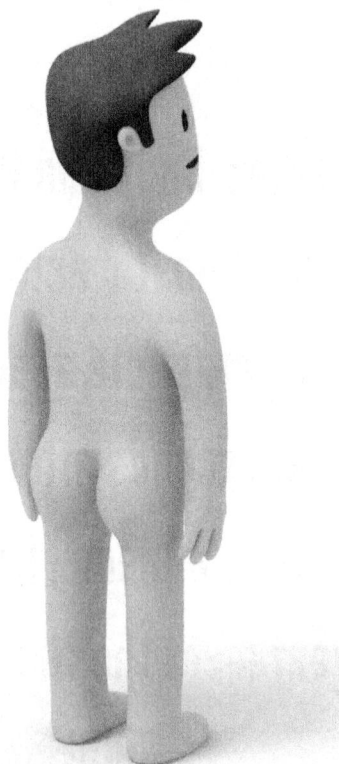

#37

From 1924 to 1992, the Winter and Summer Olympic Games were held in the same year. From now on, they are organized according to distinct cycles with an alternation of two years.

Only four athletes won medals at both the Winter and Summer Olympics, and only one of them, Christa Ludinger-Rothenburger, won medals in the same year.

#39

During the 2012 London Games, 165,000 towels were needed in the Olympic Village for just over two weeks of activity.

#40

The official languages of the Games are English and French, plus the official language of the host country.

#41

Tarzan himself competed in the Olympics, as Johnny Weissmuller, a former athlete turned actor who starred in 12 Tarzan films, won five gold medals in swimming in the 1920s.

#42

From 1912 to 1948, artists as diverse as painters, sculptors, architects, writers and musicians participated in the Olympic Games in the hope of winning medals in their respective fields.

#43

During the 1936 Games in Berlin, two Japanese pole vaulters tied for second place.

Instead of competing again, they cut the silver and bronze medals in half and combined each half to have half a silver medal and half a bronze medal.

The Olympic torch is lit in the old-fashioned way, in an ancient ceremony at the temple of Hera in Greece. Actresses dressed as Greek priestesses light the torch using a parabolic mirror and the sun's rays.

#45

From there, the torch begins its relay to the host city. It is usually carried by runners, but it has already traveled by boat, plane (and even in the Concorde), horseback, camel, via radio signal, underwater and in a canoe.

The extinguished Olympic torch has also travelled several times in space!

#46

The 2012 London Games were the first Olympic Games in which all participating countries sent female athletes.

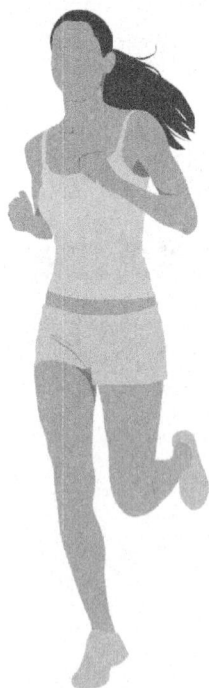

#47

The five rings of the Olympic symbol designed by Baron Pierre de Coubertin, co-founder of the modern Olympic Games, represent the five inhabited continents of the world.

#48

Waldi the dachshund was the first official Olympic mascot of the 1972 Games in Munich.

#49

The 2016 Games in Rio will mark the first time the Olympic Games are held in South America.

Rio2016™

#50

Introduced in the 1960s by the international sports authorities, the femininity test was intended to distinguish "real women" from others. It was used, until the IOC abolished it in 1999, to determine whether sportswomen were not hermaphrodites or men pretending to be women. Femininity was then certified on the basis of a gynecological examination, then chromosomal and then hormonal. Princess Anne, daughter of Queen Elizabeth II, was the only competitor who did not have to undergo this test at the Montreal Olympics in 1976.

#51

In the summer of 1984, in the Memorial Coliseum in Los Angeles, more than 92,000 people attended an opening ceremony worthy of a Hollywood production. A rocket man, Bill Suitor, flew through the air in a flying machine and landed in front of a cheering crowd. Moreover, during this celebration, a UFO appears in the sky and creates euphoria in the public. An extraordinary event not elucidated which will mark these Olympics.

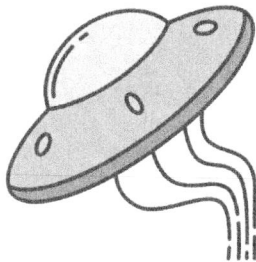

#52

During the Barcelona Olympics in 1992, the "Dream Team" was allowed to participate and basketball players such as Michael Jordan, Magic Johnson, or Patrick Ewing imposed their style of play and pulverized the other teams. This "dream team" won its eight games with a minimum of 32 points per game (44 on average). In the final on August 8, 1992, the American team won 117 to 85 against Croatia.

#53

The strongest image of the Atlanta Games is undoubtedly that of the living legend of boxing, Mohamed Ali lighting the Olympic flame with a trembling arm because of the Parkinson's disease that affects him. His gold medal won in 1960 at the Olympic Games in Rome, thrown a few years later in Ohio after being refused to serve him in a restaurant reserved for whites, is offered to him again.

#54

During the Sydney Olympic Games in 2000, an electronic anti-shark device was put in place to protect the triathlon swimmers from any attack of sharks, which are numerous in the Sydney bay. The Sharksafe company, after having received the authorization of the organizers, equipped each athlete with a 1 kilo transmitter fixed to their leg and able to repel sharks thanks to an electric field which disturbs their nervous system.

#55

Eric Moussambani, the Equatorial Guinean swimmer, became the alien of the planet Sports during the Sydney Olympics. In the Aquatic Center pool, Eric Moussambani found himself alone, his two opponents were disqualified because of a false start, he then started to swim as fast as he could but he didn't advance much! In the end, it took him 1 minute and 52 seconds to finish his race, ten seconds faster than the world record for the 200m freestyle at the time!

It is a large cast of artists exclusively "Down Under" that is invited to animate the closing ceremony of the Sydney Games. The groups "Men At Work", "Midnight Oil" and "INXS", among others, offered an Olympic performance.

But it is especially, the little darling of Australians, Kylie Minogue, who ignites the public with her version of "Dancing Queen" of ABBA that she interpreted in a fuchsia pink cabaret outfit and a feathered headband.

#57

In March 2008, the Olympic torch relay of the Beijing Olympics was launched by China on a Tiananmen Square closed to the public and highly secured to prevent demonstrators from disrupting this historic day.

Three months later the Olympic torch reached the summit of Mount Everest. To avoid any protest from pro-Tibetan activists, the Middle Kingdom deployed police forces in the area and banned all other expeditions, as in neighboring Nepal, whose access to the southern slope was closed.

#58

The maxim "the important thing is to participate" is attributed to Baron Pierre de Coubertin, historian and originator of the modern Olympic Games. However, he would never have pronounced it and this sentence so often used to comfort the losing sportsmen would be only apocryphal! In reality, he would have said, in 1908: "The important in the life it is not the triumph, but the fight, the essential it is not to have overcome but to have fought well."

LOSER

#59

For the first time in Olympic history, boxers will be able to compete at the London Games. Three weight categories are appearing: fly (45-51 kilos), light (56-60 kilos) and medium (69-75 kilos). 12 boxers are registered in each category including an Afghan.

In March 2012, the International Amateur Boxing Association (AIBA) announced that boxers would not be required to wear skirts in the ring.

#60

The Australian Olympic Committee has officially banned the use of sleeping pills for all athletes. A decision that comes after Grant Hackett, former star swimmer admitted to having developed a "heavy" addiction to drugs. However, John Coates told Bloomberg that Australian athletes have already started to practice other relaxation techniques to help them fall asleep naturally. He added, however, that athletes would be allowed to use Temazepam (a short-acting drug) in "extreme circumstances".

#61

In 1936, the German government paid about $25 million in taxes to host the Olympics in Berlin, and in 1972, when the Olympics were held in Munich, it cost nearly 70 times that amount.

#62

The budget for the Olympic Games has evolved over the course of history and depends on the local context of the host city. However, funding for the Games can be divided into two distinct budgets: the OCOG budget and the non-OCOG budget.

The OCOG budget comes primarily from the IOC's marketing outreach agreements and the Olympic Partners Program (TOP). The non-OCOG budget is under the control of the local authorities of the host city.

#63

The 2008 Olympics in Beijing, China, cost more than US$40 billion, making it the most expensive Games after the 2014 Winter Olympics in Russia, and while it was cheaper than the Russian Games, it hosted three times as many events.

#64

The 2004 Athens Games went 60 per cent over budget, leaving Greece billions of dollars in the red.

The country had hoped that the Olympics would bring longer-term gains from tourism, but many stadiums and hotel rooms remain unused.

#65

The 1980 Lake Placid Olympics went 320% over budget.

Organizers were left with an $8 million debt, and the New York state government eventually had to pay off the creditors.

#66

The most expensive Games in history were the 2014 Winter Olympics in Sochi, at more than US$50 billion, four times what Russian President Vladimir Putin had initially proposed. The original budget was $12 billion.

#67

The 1992 Winter Olympics in Albertville went 135% over budget, resulting in a $57 million deficit. The French government was forced to pay part of the bill.

The U.S. Olympic Committee provides health insurance and stipends to a limited number of competitors. without government assistance, athletes turn to prize money, apparel contracts, grants and part-time work to finance their Olympic dreams.

Even in most apparel contracts, there are provisions for reduced pay if the athlete is injured or performs below expectations.

#69

The 1992 Barcelona Olympics were hailed as one of the best and, despite being over budget, Barcelona became one of Europe's top tourist destinations. However, economists note that Barcelona, long neglected under the rule of Francisco Franco, was in the midst of a renaissance that would have occurred with or without the Olympics.

BARCELONA

#70

The Nagano Olympics in Japan went 56 per cent over their original budget. Amid allegations of corruption, entire boxes of financial documents were burned, and the total cost of Nagano is still unknown.

NAGANO
1 9 9 8

#71

Road and rail infrastructure, worth $8.7 billion, was one of the highest costs of the Sochi Olympics. The construction of the Fish stadium, where the opening and closing ceremonies will take place, cost $780 million. With a capacity of 40,000 people, this represents an average cost of $19,500 per spectator.

The International Olympic Committee has strict rules about the type and number of logos that athletes must wear.

They do this to prevent athletes from becoming human billboards, so the chances of the Olympics significantly increasing sales of a certain brand of tennis racquets, swimsuits or running shoes are slim.

#73

Approximately 47% of Olympic marketing revenue comes from broadcasting, 45% from sponsorship, 5% from ticketing and 3% from licensing.

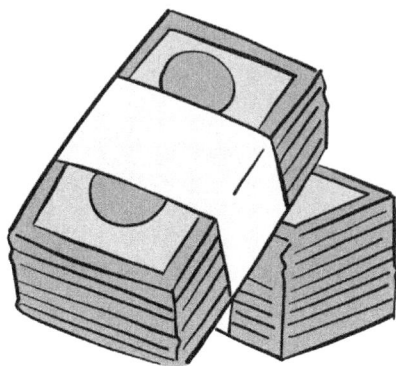

From 2005 to 2008, the International Olympic Committee (IOC) received US$270 million in ticket sales for the Olympic Games.

$

#75

The main source of revenue for the Olympic Games is the broadcast license contracts, which the International Olympic Committee (IOC) negotiates directly. The Summer Olympics generate almost twice the revenue of the Winter Olympics.

#76

The mismanagement of the 1976 Montreal Games left the city with a US$1.5 billion debt that took three decades to pay off. "The Big-O," Montreal's Olympic stadium turned baseball park, was nicknamed "The Big O-W-E."

MONTREAL

#77

The host city of the Olympic Games is chosen by vote of the members of the International Olympic Committee (IOC) at least seven years in advance.

#78

The first modern ceremony of opening, in the sense of party of openings of the Olympic games, took place in the Games of 1924 in Paris.

#79

The opening ceremony of the 2012 London Olympics cost about £27 million, making it one of the most expensive in history.

· LONDON ·

#80

The Soviet long jumper Galina Chistyakova established a new world record during the 1988 Games in Seoul by jumping 7.52 meters.

This record is still in force today.

#81

The youngest Olympic champion in track and field is Betty Robinson, an American sprinter who won the gold medal in sprinting in 1928 at the age of 16.

16

The largest time difference between first and last place in the 100-meter race at the Olympics is 0.96 seconds, which occurred at the 1904 Games in St. Louis.

During the 1984 Games in Los Angeles, the East German athlete, Juergen Hingsen, left the competition and asked for political asylum in the United States during the Games.

LOS ANGELES
CALIFORNIA

#84

At the 1996 Atlanta Games, South African marathoner Josia Thugwane became the first South African athlete to win a gold medal after the end of apartheid.

#85

At the 2000 Games in Sydney, the American athlete Marion Jones won five medals, but later she admitted to taking banned substances and lost her medals.

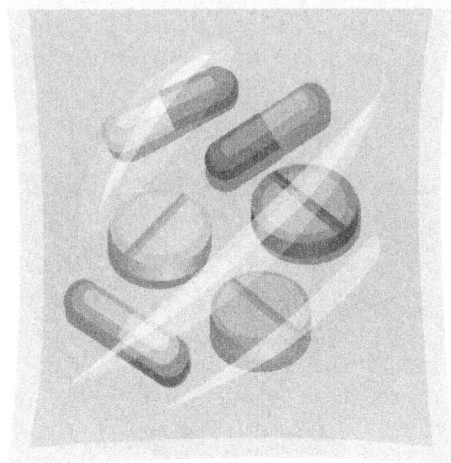

During the 2008 Games in Beijing, the Chinese gymnast Dong Fangxiao was disqualified from her medals because of a violation of the minimum age to participate in the Games. She was 14 years old at the time and the minimum age to participate is 16 years.

14

#87

Australia was the first nation to win a gold medal at the modern Olympic Games in athletics in 1896 in the 100m!

In 1908 at the London Games, the marathon runners had to stop to drink champagne and cognac offered by a spectator.

Jamaican sprinter Usain Bolt became the first man to win three consecutive 100-meter race gold medals at the Olympics in 2008, 2012 and 2016.

#90

The youngest Olympic champion in swimming is Marjorie Gestring, an American swimmer who won gold in 1936 at the age of 13.

#91

The highest number of gold medals won by a country at a single Olympic Games is 103, which was achieved by the United States at the 1984 Games in Los Angeles.

The 1904 Summer Olympics in St. Louis, U.S.A., were the first to include sports such as hammer throw, long jump and rifle shooting.

#93

The youngest participant in the modern Olympic Games was Dimitrios Loundras, a Greek gymnast who was 10 years old at the time of the 1896 Games in Athens.

In 2013, Pope Francis met with a large delegation of Olympic leaders and warned them against the over-commercialization of Olympic athletes. The pope argued that athletes are reduced to mere objects of commerce if the Games are viewed solely in economic terms. The Pope argued that this commercialization threatens the harmony of the games.

#95

The 1968 marathon runner, Kip Keino of Kenya, ran the race sick and not having eaten for days. He nevertheless won the gold medal.

#96

In 1988, diver Greg Louganis hit his head on the edge of the board at the Seoul Games, but continued diving and won the gold medal.

#97

While the organizers of the London Games promised to use the Olympics to revitalize east London (an area of historic socio-economic deprivation), they had to bulldoze several local businesses to make way for the new venues. and despite a commitment to create 20,000 jobs in the area, less than half of them have been created.

WORK

Beijing's 423 million U.S. dollar Bird's Nest Stadium costs 11 million U.S. dollars a year to maintain.

Today, tourists can take a Segway tour of the Olympic Stadium for $20.

#99

The researchers note that there are ways to make the Olympics a financial success for a host city, all by building on existing facilities to host events and using the Olympics as a catalyst to build long-term infrastructure projects that would be needed with or without the games.

#100

Did you like this book?
Discover our other creations

Click on the QR code below :

Printed in Great Britain
by Amazon

THE BEST
100
short stories

You like the top 100?

You'll love the 100 short stories series.
L'Atelier has the best selection for you.

To be leafed through alone or shared with friends
these anecdotes will develop your knowledge and
make you have a good time.

A fun way to learn
and to awaken your curiosity.

ISBN 9798385775637

9798385 775637

L'atelier